Can We Go Outside to Play Today?

Julia A. Royston

Illustrated by Cameron T. Wilson

ROYSTON
Publishing

BK Royston Publishing LLC

P. O. Box 4321

Jeffersonville, IN 47131

http://www.bkroystonpublishing.com

bkroystonpublishing@gmail.com

Copyright 2020

All Rights Reserved. No part of this book may be reproduced, stored in a retrieval system, or transmitted by any means without the written permission of the author.

Cover and Illustrations: Cameron T. Wilson

ISBN: 978-1-951941-51-2

Printed in the USA

Dedication

This is dedicated to all of us who have experienced a unique time of staying inside. #inthistogether #stayinside

Acknowledgement

I thank you Father for giving me another opportunity to write and entrusting this gift to me. Bless the people who will purchase, read and pass along some of the knowledge located in this book.

To my husband, Brian K. Royston, the love of my life, for loving and cheering me on so much that I can be and do all that the Father has placed in me. You are the wind, air, breath and engine beneath my wings. I love you...

To my Mom, my greatest supporter and best friend. To my Dad, who is in heaven, that I know is proud of me and always encouraged me to go for it. Thanks to all of the rest of my family for their love and support.

A special thank you to Rev. and Mrs. Claude R. Royston for their love and support.

Thank you to Cameron Wilson who did another excellent job illustrating this book.

Julia A. Royston

Introduction

I had such high hopes for 2020. It was going to be a year like no other. It didn't disappoint. So many things happened that hadn't happened before in my life time or my parents. What do you do when something happens that you don't expect? You make the most of it. You listen to your parents. You protect each other. You remember all of the things that are important like Love, Family and Writing. These are things that I found to be most important in my life right now.

So this book is not to scare or create more trauma, but is designed to help you to have a conversation, let out your feelings and hopefully, feel better along with your parents, friends, teachers and counselors.

Enjoy the story. Stay Safe. Live Your Best Life. Be Your Best Self.

Julia A. Royston.

Can we go outside to play today?
Mommy said, "No."
Daddy said, "Stay
In the house and play."

"Why? Sister and I will be okay!"

Mommy said, "The people outside maybe sick. So to be safe, in the house we must stay."

Wash your hands
even more today.
Stay inside,
It's the safe way.

The trees are green.
The flowers are in bloom.
There's the swings
and the slide.
Go with us, it's just outside.

Your room is fine.
Those toys are too.
People may get near you.
It's not safe, for me or you.

Suddenly, there is a noise.
On the TV, broken glass.
What's happening now?
We almost hate to ask.

Someone got hurt.
No one we know.
The crowds are huge!
So can we go?

It must be safe now,
There are others outside.
The playground is waiting,
The house we still abide.

Daddy's angry.
Mommy's crying.
We'll be safe.
We promise and
we're not lying.

We believe you and
know you speak the truth.
It's only because we love you,
That we all stay under
this roof.

We've got on our mask.
We'll do as you ask.
Whatever you say,
Just can we play
outside today?

The days went slowly by,
We played, they worked all inside.
Until Daddy said, "Today, we will try."
He opened the door and we all went outside.

We had such fun,
On the swings and the slide.
After being in the house
so long,
We were finally safe outside.

Time for bed,
it's almost dark.
Sweet dreams come easy,
from our time in the park.
Our family together,
in the house we reside.
Hopefully tomorrow,
another day outside.

I trust that you enjoyed the book, "Can We Go Outside and Play Today?" It has been a hard and confusing time in 2020, but together we will continue to make it through.

Vocabulary

Play

Outside

Inside

Wash Hands

Safe

Mask

In the story, there were three ways that the family did to stay safe.

1

2.

3.

Send your answers to readingprogram@roystonroyalbookstore.com for a chance to win a prize.

Draw a picture of some of the things that your family did to have fun and stay safe while staying inside at home. Email this picture with your parents' permission to readingprogram@bkroystonfoundation.org

For more information about Julia Royston and to purchase more of her books, visit: www.roystonroyalbookstore.com

www.ingramcontent.com/pod-product-compliance
Lightning Source LLC
Chambersburg PA
CBHW061400090426
42743CB00002B/86